The Laughing Soldier

The British Armed Forces
Jokebook

Illustrated by The Comic Stripper

CASEMATE

Newbury & Philadelphia

First published in Great Britain in 2010 by
Casemate Publishers
17 Cheap Street, Newbury, Berkshire RG14 5DD, United Kingdom
and in the United States by
Casemate Publishers
908 Darby Road, Havertown, PA 19083, USA

ISBN 978-1-61200-0381

Page layout by Mousemat Design Limited, Orpington, Kent, UK
Edited by Ruth Sheppard
Printed and bound by Gutenberg Press Ltd, Malta
Front cover image © Getty Images

10 9 8 7 6 5 4 3 2 1

For a complete catalogue of all books published by Casemate, please contact:

UNITED KINGDOM
Casemate Publishers
Tel: (01635) 231091 Fax: (01635) 41619
E-mail: casemate-uk@casematepublishing.co.uk
Website: www.casematepublishing.co.uk

NORTH AMERICA
Casemate Publishers
Tel: (610) 853 9131 Fax: (610) 853 9146
E-mail: casemate@casematepublishing.com
Website: www.casematepublishing.com

ABOUT PROJECT 65 – THE VETERANS CHARITY

Project 65 – The Veterans Charity – was founded in 2008 to raise funds for the care and support of wounded Armed Forces veterans and their families.

There are hundreds of different issues faced by UK Armed Forces veterans and families of the Armed Forces community. Project 65 focuses on being able to help fund the vital care and support available for every issue faced by those associated with forces life.

These issues include:

* Treatment and rehabilitation following wounding or injury
* Mental health
* Illness
* Financial support
* Housing
* Education
* Employment
* Bereavement counselling
* Childcare
* Mobility
* Family welfare

Every pound raised by Project 65 – The Veterans Charity will make a difference to the amount of money we can provide for our chosen beneficiaries and will enable them to continue providing the vital care and support they give to individuals and families affected by injury or trauma as a result of service in the UK armed forces. These do not just include the current and recent conflicts in Iraq or

Afghanistan but also Kosovo, Bosnia, Northern Ireland, The Falklands, Borneo, Aden, Korea and of course World War II.

More information about the charity and how you can help or get involved can be found at www.project65.net

The Laughing Soldier grew from our love of the legendary "military sense of humour", the unique ability to find humour in the toughest of situations but also for some of the sharpest humour there has ever been.

Look at the greats of comedy – *The Goon Show*, *Dad's Army*, *Blackadder* or *Monty Python* – many of the cast members and writers had a military background and some of the shows were even given a military theme or setting.

The Laughing Soldier has three simple aims:

- To provide a source of laughter when it's needed most
- To give the caring and supportive British public a chance to send their messages of support directly to those on the front lines
- To raise funds to help the care and support of veterans and forces families through Project 65 – The Veterans Charity.

There is an almost overwhelming feeling of pride amongst the British public for what our armed forces do around the world to help protect communities from tyranny and oppression as well as ensure our country remains a safe place for us all.

We often feel that the words "thank you" could never be enough to express our gratitude and pride for everyone that has served in the Royal Navy, Army or Royal Air Force, both now and in the past. We sincerely hope that *The Laughing Soldier* will bring a smile and a laugh to those who are serving around the world and that the many messages of support will provide an insight into just how much pride, gratitude and respect there is for our Armed Forces.

Foreword by Al Murray – The Pub Landlord

Laughter finds its way into the strangest places. It permeates every aspect of life, so it should be no surprise that here's a joke book full of military humour. It can be a very particular kind of humour, the banter you'd find among mates, the kind of in-jokes, barbs and gags that to outsiders seem incomprehensible; the slogans chalked onto the sides of the gliders found outside Arnhem in 1944 stating things like "We are the Al Capone Gang" and "Up the Fräuleins' skirts" were met with bafflement by the enemy (and not just because they were humourless Germans). And when the Royal Dragoon Guards crashed the MOD's computer system with their Amarillo spoof, someone was laughing (though probably not the MOD).

But mainly I hope that this book with all its jokes will put a smile on the face of the people doing what they're doing so we that don't have to do what they're doing, because that, in the end, is what it boils down to.

Cheers!
Al Murray

Foreword by former Royal Marine Mark Ormrod

Due to the harsh nature of life in the military, especially during times of conflicts, a good sense of humour is a key aspect to getting through the tough times that face all of our servicemen and women. Being able to tell a joke or "crack a funny" when morale is low can help even the worst of situations seem that little bit better. Our armed forces are well known for their sense of humour especially in the face of adversity. Humour was a key factor for me when I got injured right from the point of being cas-evaced up until the low points in my rehabilitation and even still today, so remember when you're feeling low and you're sick and tired of everything, laughter is the best medicine.

Mark Ormrod is one of the UK's best-known former servicemen. Mark joined the Royal Marines and went on his first operational tour in Afghanistan in 2007. Just eight weeks into his tour he was caught in a landmine blast which tore off both legs and his right arm. Mark's amazing sense of humour can be summed up with his first comment after learning of his appalling injuries: "So my dancing days are over then?"

A vicar looked over a garden wall and saw a
gardener working among a fine display of
flowers, fruit and vegetables.
"Isn't it wonderful what God can do in a
garden?" he remarked.
"Yes," said the gardener, "but you should
have seen what it was like when he had it to
himself."

**With very best wishes to everyone serving
far from home this Christmas.**

Alan Titchmarsh, television presenter and
celebrity gardener

The reason the Army, Royal Navy, Air Force
and Royal Marines squabble among
themselves is that they don't speak the same
language. For example, take a simple phrase
like "Secure the Building":
The Army will put guards around the place.
The Royal Navy will turn out the lights and
lock the doors.
The RAF will take out a five-year lease with
an option to buy.
The Royal Marines will kill everybody inside
and make a command post.

With love to you all.

Janice

The kid next door just challenged me to a water fight. Typing this waiting for the kettle to boil!

Blue Skies and Soft Landings.

Charlie Marsden

Three infantry squaddies were captured by Taliban terrorists. They were buried up to their necks in sand, just within reach of a lovely stretch of water.

The most senior said to the others, "They want us to suffer from thirst, whilst baking in the sun close to water. Don't give them the satisfaction . . . . Don't give in."

After hours of this, the terrorists sitting in the shade watching, noticed that the squaddies' heads were moving in time, from side to side.

One of the terrorists said. "Hakim, go and see what they are doing."

Hakim returned looking bewildered and said, "Malik, they are singing?"

Malik, stunned, said "Singing, what are they singing?"

"They are singing . . . 'Ooooooooh I dooo like to be beside the seaside!'"

You have all shown the world the true meaning of "Selfless Commitment, Courage, Discipline, Integrity, Loyalty and Respect for Others." Your individual courage is something the United Kingdom is very proud of. Thank you from the bottom of my heart for being the "True Heroes" that you all are. Take care, stay safe and keep smiling always!

Anita Cowgill-Taylor

A class of children were asked by their teacher to think of stories with a good moral! One child said to the teacher, "My grandad was going to the market and he was collecting eggs and my nan said 'Use the three baskets over there.' But he only used one basket, and on the way to market all the eggs broke! The moral is don't put all your eggs in one basket!"

"Great!" said the teacher.

Another child said, "My dad was going shopping and he noticed a little old lady whose car had a flat tyre, so he stopped and changed it for her! The next day the little old lady was with her son (who was a rich man), when they saw my dad outside the job centre and the son offered him a job! The moral is one good turn deserves another!"

"Well done!" said the teacher.

Little Bobby sat in the corner. He piped up very excitedly, holding up his arm, wriggling to get the teacher's attention, "Go on then Bobby!" said the teacher.

"Miss, Miss, my uncle is in the army and he was in an aeroplane going to Afghanistan and the plane got hit and he put on his parachute and grabbed his gun and a bottle of whisky and he jumped! On the way down in the dark and a blistering sandstorm, he drank the whisky. When he landed he was surrounded by 150 of the fiercest Taliban fighters. He shot 50 dead and then, out of bullets, he killed another 50 with the butt of his GPMG. THE FINAL 50 HE KILLED WITH HIS BARE HANDS, FEET AND TEETH!"
"Wow," the teacher said "but what on earth is the moral of the story?"
"Don't mess with my Uncle Scott when he has had a drink!"

To all out there in any theatre, keep your chins up and heads down. You are doing a sterling job for which we all are very, very grateful!

Ali Weatherstone, presenter, BFBS Radio

Did you hear about the Brummy who fought in Vietnam? He kept getting flashbacks to when he lived in Birmingham!

Sometimes people say comedians have a difficult job, but we all know it's nothing to what you guys do.

Milton Jones, comedian

A gorilla walked into a bar and ordered a pint of beer.
The barman served him with a frothing pint of real ale and said "That'll be £5 please."
The gorilla handed over a five-pound note.
The barman said: "We don't get many gorillas in here," to which the gorilla replied,
"I'm not surprised at £5 a pint."

**With every best wish to our men and women at the sharp end.
We are all very proud of you.**

Alex Cunningham, Labour MP for Stockton North

A man wins the National Lottery and scoops £8 million.

The press call on him at home and ask him, "What's it like to win 8 million pounds? Will it make any difference to your job as a cleaner with Asda?"

He says, "You bet your life it will, I have told them to stuff their ruddy job and I'm going to enjoy myself from now on."

The journalist says, "And what about your wife? Will it make any difference to her as a cleaner at Tesco?"

He says, "Why? Has she won the lottery as well?"

We should all be grateful to those who put their own lives at risk for our country.

The Rt Hon Greg Knight MP, Chairman of the Procedure Committee, Chairman of the Parliamentary Historic Vehicles Group

A father and his young son were in a long queue at the post office. In front of them was a woman who frankly could do with losing a few pounds! Suddenly her mobile phone rang. "Watch out Dad," said the boy "she's reversing!"

Best wishes to you and everyone out there.

Alex Lester, BBC Radio 2

British: "Please divert your course 15 degrees to the South to avoid collision."

Americans: "Recommend you divert your course 15 degrees to the North to avoid a collision."

British: "Negative. You will have to divert your course 15 degrees to the South to avoid a collision."

Americans: "This is the Captain of a US Navy ship. I say again, divert YOUR course."

British: "No, I say again, you divert YOUR course."

Americans: "THIS IS THE AIRCRAFT CARRIER USS LINCOLN, THE SECOND LARGEST SHIP IN THE UNITED STATES' ATLANTIC FLEET. WE ARE ACCOMPANIED BY THREE DESTROYERS, THREE CRUISERS, AND NUMEROUS SUPPORT VESSELS. I DEMAND THAT YOU CHANGE YOUR COURSE 15 DEGREES NORTH – I SAY AGAIN, THAT'S ONE FIVE DEGREES NORTH – OR COUNTER-MEASURES WILL BE UNDERTAKEN TO ENSURE THE SAFETY OF THIS SHIP."

British: "This is a lighthouse. Your call!"

We owe such a debt of gratitude to all of you serving overseas to protect our freedom. We can't begin to understand how hard it is for you to be away from your families and loved ones and Christmas makes that absence even harder. I hope that this book will make you smile and, if just for a short while, give you a welcome break from your duties and responsibilities. I commend you for the work you are doing so that we can have peace of mind. Thank you.

Julian Huppert, MP for Cambridge

Adam says to Eve – or perhaps Eve
said to Adam,
"Do you love me?"
The answer, after looking around
for a moment,
"Who else?"

Peter Bottomley, MP for Worthing West

Two hunters are out in the woods when one of them collapses. He doesn't seem to be breathing and his eyes are glazed. The other guy whips out his phone and calls the emergency services.

He gasps: "My friend is dead! What can I do?"

The operator says: "Calm down, I can help. First, let's make sure he's dead."

There is a silence, then a shot is heard.

Back on the phone, the guy says: "OK, now what?"

I wanted to send a huge thank you for all the work you're doing to keep us safe. I know that if you're anything like my brother who spent 22 years in the Signals, you'd much rather that I was sending you black pudding, scotch pies or some other luxury from home, but hopefully this book will help give you some smiles this Xmas!

Mike Crockart, MP for Edinburgh West

Hedgehogs? Why can't they just share the hedge?

Sincere thanks and very best wishes to each and every one of you.

Rt Hon George Osborne MP, Chancellor of the Exchequer

A bloke walks into his local NAAFI, sits down and says to the bartender, "Quick, pour me twelve vodkas."
So the bartender pours him twelve shots and the bloke starts shooting them back and finishes all in twelve seconds.
The bartender says to the bloke, "Hang on, you are drinking those drinks really fast."
The bloke says, "Well, you would be drinking really fast too if you had what I've got."
The bartender says, "What've you got?"
The bloke says, "75 pence."

Please enjoy this joke and all the others! I hope that they will cheer you guys and gals up, who are doing a sterling job on behalf of the British people. We are so proud and grateful and will always remember your service.

Alun Cairns MP, Vale of Glamorgan

A farmer named Sid was overseeing his stock in a remote moorland pasture in North Yorkshire when suddenly, out of a cloud of dust, a brand-new Porsche Cayenne advanced toward him.

The driver, a young man in a Paul Smith suit, Gucci shoes, RayBan sunglasses and YSL tie, leaned out the window and asked the farmer, "If I tell you exactly how many cows and calves you have in your herd, will you give me a calf?"

Sid looks at the man, obviously a new-age yuppie, then looks at his peacefully grazing stock and calmly answers, "Sure, why not?"

The yuppie parks his car, whips out his Dell notebook computer, connects it to his Cingular RAZR V3 cell phone, and backup wifi dongle, and surfs to a NASA page on the Internet, where he calls up a GPS satellite to get an exact fix on his location, which he then feeds to another NASA satellite that scans the area as an ultra-high-resolution photo.

The young man then opens the digital photo in Adobe Photoshop and exports it to an image processing facility in Hamburg, Germany.

Within seconds, he receives an email on his Palm Pilot that the image has been processed and the data stored. He then accesses an MS-SQL database through an ODBC connected Excel spreadsheet, with email, on his Blackberry and, after a few minutes, receives a response. Just for backup it also arrives on his iPhone and iPad for good measure.

Finally, he prints out a full-colour, 150-page report on his hi-tech, miniaturized HP LaserJet printer, turns to the farmer and says, "You have exactly 1,586 cows and calves."

"That's right. Well, I guess you can take one of my calves," says Sid.

He looks on with amusement as the young man selects one of the animals and stuffs it into the back of his car.

Then Sid says to the young man, "Hey, if I can tell you exactly what your business is, will you give me back my calf?

The young man thinks about it for a second and then says, "Okay, why not?"

"You're a management consultant." says Sid.

"Wow! That's correct," says the yuppie, "but how on earth did you guess that?"

"No guessing required," answered the farmer, "you showed up here even though nobody called you; you want to get paid for an answer I already knew, to a question I never asked. You used millions of pounds worth of equipment trying to show me how much smarter than me you are; and you don't know a thing about how working people make a living – or about cows, for that matter. This is a herd of sheep . . .

. . . now give me back my dog!"

All of us right-minded people back home appreciate fully what you all do, and thank you sincerely for doing what you do, professionally and with spirit and vigour.

Karl McCartney JP, MP for Lincoln

I think out of all the planets in our solar system, the name Saturn has to be my favourite. It's just got a certain ring to it.

Good luck for you and all your families.

Jim Barker

Paddy and his wife are lying in bed and the neighbours' dog is barking like mad in the garden.

Paddy says, "To hell with this!"

He gets out of bed and storms out the room.

He comes back upstairs five minutes later and his wife asks "What did you do?"

Paddy replies, "I've put the dog in our garden. Let's see how they like it!"

Very proud to be British and I'm proud of you all. Thank you for the amazing job you are doing out there.

Mark Pilton, Ex RN

There once was an inflatable boy called Timmy, he went to an inflatable school with inflatable children and inflatable teachers. Actually everything in his world was inflatable.

One day Timmy found a pin. Timmy being Timmy then proceeded to puncture things. He started small, popping a cherry. He quickly moved on to bigger things – first he popped the bullies, then the teachers and his friends, until finally he popped his own school.

The next day, once everything had repaired, he was called in to see the head master, who started by saying, "Not only have you let me down, you've let yourself down and you've let the whole school down!"

I've just got back from Herrick 12 and think that this is an absolutely fantastic idea. Although the sense of humour and camaraderie that British squaddies have is second to none, there are times when you just want to be on your own and that's when something to put a smile on your face is most needed.

Sgt D. N. Davies, R Signals

A woman was putting together a puzzle. She was really stumped and very frustrated, so she decided to ask her husband for help.

"It's supposed to be a tiger!" she cried.

"Put the Frosties back in the box love!" said her husband.

God bless and thank you!

Anon

Dear John's revenge:

The soldier was annoyed and upset when his girl wrote breaking off their engagement and asking for her photograph back.

He went out and collected from his friends all the unwanted photographs of women that he could find, bundled them all together and sent them back with a note saying, "I regret to inform you that I can't remember which one is you – please keep your photo and return the others."

A BFBS Listener

I banged my head last night so I put some margarine on it. Woke up this morning and I can't believe it's not better.

John Marable, Ex Army Sgt of 22 years

A woman was visiting her husband in hospital following major surgery. As the man slowly woke from the anaesthetic he looked at his wife and muttered, "You're beautiful!"

He then fell asleep again.

Two hours later he woke once more and, looking at his wife again said, "You look nice."

"What happened to beautiful then?" said his wife.

"The drugs are wearing off!" replied the man.

Stay safe and stay smiling!

Dave Mitchell

A carpenter slipped whilst using his new band saw and cut off all his fingers. He screamed and ran out of his workshop towards the nearest hospital.

Eventually he was seen by a nurse, who says "Without your fingers, we can't do much for you I'm afraid. Go back and get them and we can sew them back on."

Reluctantly and in considerable agony, the man leaves for home. After several hours he returns to the hospital. The nurse asks him for his severed fingers.

"I couldn't pick them up!" says the man.

With respect, thanks and best wishes.

Sarah Jackson

At 7am one morning a man stumbles, blind drunk, with lipstick on his face and collar, into his kitchen and is confronted by his furious wife.

"I suppose there's a good reason why you have come home in that state?" she shouts.

"Breakfast!" replies the man.

My thoughts are with you all every day. Stay safe!

Brian Smith, Ex RAF

An Essex girl is involved in a car crash and when the paramedics arrive, one asks her,
"What's your name love?"
"Sharon." replies the girl.
On closer inspection the paramedic notices a lot of blood on the girl's clothing. "Where are you bleeding from Sharon?" he enquires.
"Romford!" says Sharon.

We're all right with you guys!

Phil Stevens

A blonde walks into a library and asks the librarian, "Can I have a Big Mac meal please?"

"Miss," replies the stunned librarian, "THIS is a LIBRARY!"

"So sorry," whispers the girl, "can I have a Big Mac meal please?"

This made me giggle and I hope it brings a smile to your faces. THANK YOU!

Zoë Davies

These 3D TVs are amazing!
Fell asleep during the Liverpool
match, and when I woke up, my
wallet had been nicked.

Charlie Marsden

Manchester United sign a new hotshot striker
from Rwanda and in his first game he scores
a hat-trick of brilliant goals.
He phones his mum as soon as the game
finishes, to tell her his news. She starts
crying as soon as he speaks.
He asks her what is wrong, and she says,
"This morning your sister was attacked by a
gang of thugs and your little brother was
savaged by a pack of wild dogs. Then your
father was shot by a sniper and I was mugged
and beaten while on my way to the store!"
Heartbroken, the footballer says, "Mum, I'm
so sorry!"
"You should be!" shouts his now very angry
mother. "It's all your fault we had to move to
Manchester!"

Swift and Bold!

John Jones

Police cordoned off Liverpool city centre this morning when a suspicious object was discovered in a car. It later turned out to be a tax disc.

Support you all the way guys, all the best and keep up the fantastic work.

Joe Spooner

How do you annoy Lady Gaga?
Poke her face!

**My friends and I like this joke.
We hope you do too!**

Henry Sullivan, 6

A lost sales rep stops to ask a passing Marine for directions. "Excuse me," says the rep, "what's the quickest way to Exeter?"
The Marine thinks for a moment and then asks, "Are you walking or driving?"
"I'm driving," replies the man.
"Yep. That's the quickest way!" says the Marine.

Head down, arse up lads and lasses!

Matt Fullard, Ex Army

Two cows are in a field. One says to the other, "What do you make of all this mad cow's disease then?" "Doesn't bother me mate," says the other, "I'm a penguin!"

Dean Grimshawe

Thieves have broken into Manchester City's trophy room and stolen everything. Police are looking for a man with a pale blue carpet!

Mark Pilton

A milkman is making a delivery to the last house on his round and he sees a note on the door that says, "45 gallons of milk, please." Curious, he knocks on the door and a blonde woman answers.

"Is this note correct?" he asks.

"Yes," replies the blonde, "it said on a TV programme that bathing in milk is really good for your skin."

"Do you want it pasteurized?" asks the milkman.

"No, just up to my neck will be fine." says the woman.

Take care and come home safe.

Cheryl Wallis

Two fleas are planning a short break to the other side of the house. "Shall we hop or take the cat?"

Thank you for your courage, sacrifice and endeavours. God bless.

Valerie Whitaker, former Wren

Quasimodo asks Esmerelda one day whether he is the ugliest man alive. "Why don't you ask the magic mirror?" she suggests.
So Quasimodo climbs the stairs to ask the mirror. He returns looking sad and confused. "Who is Iain Dowie?" he asks.

I am immensely proud of all of you and my thoughts are with you every day. I hope that this book will bring you a smile or a giggle at the end of a tough day!

Danny Greeno – CEO, Project 65 – The Veterans Charity

A snail goes into a pub, slides up the stool and onto the bar.

He says to the barman, "Pint of lager and packet of crisps please mate."

The barman says, "Sorry we don't serve snails."

Snail says, "Aww c'mon, just a pint of lager and a packet of crisps, please."

The barman says again, "Look I've told you we DON'T serve snails."

The snail tries once more, "Please mate, pint of lager and a packet of crisps, that's all."

The Barman is fed up now and gets hold of the snail and chucks him out of the door saying, "How many more times, we don't serve snails!"

A week passes by, the pub door opens, the snail slides up the bar stool and says, "What did you do that for?"

With best wishes to all our servicemen and women . . . always thinking of you.

Lorraine Weights

As a family, we try to keep up with technology, so I bought my son an iPod, my daughter an iPhone, and myself an iPad. Felt sorry for the wife so I bought her an iron. That's when she kicked off!

Charlie Marsden

It was a dark, stormy night. A marine was on guard duty for the very first time.

A general stepped out taking his dog for a walk. The nervous young private snapped to attention, made a perfect salute, and snapped out, "Sir, Good Evening, Sir!" The general, out for some relaxation, returned the salute and said, "Good evening soldier, nice night, isn't it?" Well it wasn't a nice night, but the private wasn't going to disagree with the general, so he saluted again and replied, "Sir, Yes Sir!"

The general continued, "You know there's something about a stormy night that I find soothing, it's really relaxing. Don't you agree?"

The private didn't agree, but then the private was just a private, so he responded, "Sir, Yes Sir!"

The general pointed at his dog and said, "This is a golden retriever, the best type of dog to train."

The private glanced at the dog, saluted yet again, and said, "Sir, Yes Sir!"

The general continued, "I got this dog for my wife."

The private simply said, "Good trade, Sir!"

As one who has served I send my best wishes to each and every one of you for a safe tour.

Paul Cavendish

A man walks into a petrol station and says, "Can I have a Kit Kat Chunky?"

The lady behind the counter gets a Kit Kat Chunky and brings it back to him.

"No," says the man, "I wanted a normal Kit Kat, Fatty."

Mark Ormrod, Former RM

Jim Davidson was standing outside his car urinating in a lay-by when two policeman spot him and go to investigate. "Is this your car, Sir?" says the first officer.

"Yes officer."

"I see. Have you been drinking?"

"I'm not gonna lie officer, I'm plastered! I've had a real good night!"

"Well, regretfully sir you're under arrest, and you'll need to accompany us to the station."

"Really?" says Jim. "Well in that case can you give me a couple of ticks so I can tell the chauffeur where I'm going?"

Dean Grimshawe

During World War II, when the Germans bombed the British ducked; when the British bombed the Germans ducked; and when the Americans bombed EVERYONE ducked.

Please pass on my thanks to all those who are fighting and have fought in past conflicts, for everything they have done and continue to do. Each day I thank God that I have my freedom because of them.

Andy Lewis

The OC called the CSM in. "Sgt Major, I just got a telegram that Private Martin's mother died yesterday. Better go tell him and send him in to see me."
So the CSM calls for his morning formation and lines up all the troops. "Listen up men," says the CSM. "Johnson, report to the mess hall for KP. Jones, report to Personnel to sign some papers. The rest of you men report to the ranges. Oh by the way, Martin, your mother died, report to the commander."
Later that day the OC called the Sergeant into his office. "CSM that was a pretty cold way to inform Martin his mother had died. Couldn't you be a bit more tactful, next time?"
"Yes, sir," answered the CSM.
A few months later, the OC called the CSM in again with, "CSM, I just got a telegram that Private Phillips' mother died. You'd better go tell him and send him in to see me but this time be more tactful."
So the CSM calls for his morning parade. "Ok, men, fall in and listen up. Everybody with a mother, take two steps forward . . . Not so fast, Phillips!"

Chris Flanigan

Dear Tech Support,

Last year I upgraded from "Boyfriend" to "Husband"
and noticed a distinct slowdown in overall system
performance – particularly in the "Flower" and
"Jewellery" applications, which operated flawlessly
under "Boyfriend".
In addition, "Husband" uninstalled many other
valuable programs, such as "Romance" and "Personal
Attention" and then installed undesirable programs
such as "The Ashes", "Football" and "Golf Clubs".
"Conversation" no longer runs, and "Housecleaning"
simply crashes the system.
I've tried running "Nagging" to fix these problems,
but to no avail.
What can I do?
Signed,
Desperate

Dear Desperate,

First keep in mind that "Boyfriend" is an Entertainment Package, while "Husband" is an Operating System.
Please enter the command: "http://www.IThoughtYou LovedMe.html" and try to download "Tears" and don't forget to install the "Guilt" update.
If that application works as designed, "Husband" should then automatically run the applications "Jewellery" and "Flowers".
But remember, overuse of the above application can cause "Husband" to default to "Grumpy Silence", "Happy Hour" or "Beer".
"Beer" is a very bad program that will download the "Snoring Loudly" Beta.
Whatever you do, DO NOT install "Mother-in-law" (it runs a virus in the background that will eventually seize control of all your system resources).
Also, do not attempt to reinstall the "Boyfriend" program. These are unsupported applications and will crash "Husband".
In summary, "Husband" is a great program, but it does have limited memory and cannot learn new applications quickly.
You might consider buying additional software to improve memory and performance. We recommend "Food" and "Hot Lingerie".
Good Luck,
Tech support

Anita Taylor

Two oranges walk into a bar,
one turns to the other and says
"You're round."

Ruth, BFBS Northern Ireland

Who is the coolest guy in the hospital?
The ultra-sound guy.

When the ultra-sound guy is off, who is the
coolest guy in the hospital?
The hip replacement man.

Thank you very much, I'm here all week!

Jonny O'Callaghan

A wife woke in the middle of the night to find her husband missing from bed. She got out of bed and checked around the house. She heard sobbing from the basement.
After turning on the light and descending the stairs, she found her husband curled up into a little ball, sobbing.
"Honey, what's wrong?" she asked, worried about what have could upset him so much.
"Remember, twenty years ago, I got you pregnant? And your father said I had to marry you or go to jail?"
"Yes, of course," she replied.
"Well, I would have been released tonight."

Jake Fuller

A cosmetics company has developed a new aftershave that makes men irresistible to women. It smells like a wallet.

The Rt Hon Greg Knight MP

A woman bought herself some new cosmetics, which claimed to make the user look years younger.
After applying the "miracle" products she asked her husband, "Honestly, what age would you say I am?"
Looking carefully, he replied, "Judging from your skin, 25; your hair, 20; and your figure, 18."
"Oh, you flatterer!" she gushed.
"Wait . . ." he interrupted. "I haven't added them up yet."

My thoughts are with you all every day. As an Army wife I know what you go through. Stay safe!

Michelle

A woman was going on a first date with a man she'd been attracted to for a long time. She was understandably very nervous. When he came to her door, she started to feel gassy and realized the chilli she'd had for lunch had been a bad idea. Being a gentlemen, he carefully put her in the car and shut the door for her. As he walked around to his side, she farted loudly and quickly opened the window and began fanning. She was horrified when he got in and pointed to the back seat saying, "Have you met Ruth and Bob?"

Phil Stevens

A farmhand walked into a barn to find the farmer doing a striptease. "What are you doing?" said the farmhand.

"Oh," says the farmer, "thing is me and the wife haven't been getting on too well and the counsellor said I should do something to a tractor!"

The British fighting man – best in the world! Thanks for proving it again and again.

Tim, Ex 2 Para 1982

A guy walks into a psychiatrist's office covered only in clingfilm. He says to the doctor, "I've felt so weird lately, Doc, can you tell me what's wrong?"
The doctor replied, "Well, I can clearly see your nuts!"

Matt Fullard

How do you keep a blonde
at home?
Build a circular driveway.

Thank you for your service. Keep safe.

Mark Pritchard

A man placed some flowers on the grave of his dearly departed mother and started back toward his car when his attention was diverted by another man kneeling at a grave. The man seemed to be praying with profound intensity and kept repeating, "Why did you have to die? Why did you have to die?" The first man approached him and said, "Sir, I don't wish to interfere with your private grief, but this demonstration of pain is more than I've ever seen before. For whom do you mourn so deeply? A child? A parent?" The mourner took a moment to collect himself, then replied, "My wife's first husband."

God bless you all.

Diana Moore

What did the fish say when he hit the wall?
DAM!

Why do Eskimos wash their clothes in Tide?
Because it's too cold "out tide"!

What do you call a boomerang that doesn't
come back?
A stick!

Why did the stoplight turn red?
Wouldn't you if you had to change in the
middle of the street?

What is the difference between
a woman and a magnet?
Magnets have a positive side!

John Jones

What has four legs and an arm?
A happy Rottweiler.

Living with pride for all of you. Come home safe!

Michaela Jones

The fight we had last night was my fault, my wife asked me what was on the TV, and I said "Dust."

We're all thinking of you and sending you the very best. Keep safe and happy.

Maria Smith

As the family gathered for a big dinner together, the youngest son announced that he had just signed up at an army recruiter's office.

There were audible gasps around the table then some laughter, as his older brothers shared their disbelief that he could handle this new situation.

"Oh, come on, stop messing about," snickered one. "You didn't really do that, did you?"

"You would never get through basic training," scoffed another.

The new recruit looked to his mother for help, but she was just gazing at him.

When she finally spoke, she simply asked, "Do you really plan to make your own bed every morning?"

I don't know anyone who agrees with war but I know many who are very proud of you all. Stay safe!

David Andrews

A teacher asked her class one day to write about something unusual that happened during the past week. Little Tommy got up to read his. "My dad fell in a very deep hole last week . . ." he began.

"Oh no!" shrieked the teacher. "Is he all right now?"

"He must be," said Tommy, "he stopped shouting for help yesterday."

I am truly grateful for the freedom and safety we have thanks to our troops!

Paul Gray

A man comes home from an exhausting day at work, plops down on the couch in front of the television, and tells his wife, "Get me a beer before it starts." The wife sighs and gets him a beer.

Fifteen minutes later, he says, "Get me another beer before it starts." She looks cross, but fetches another beer and slams it down next to him.

He finishes that beer and a few minutes later says, "Quick, get me another beer, it's going to start any minute."

The wife is furious. She yells at him "Is that all you're going to do tonight? Drink beer and sit in front of that TV? You're nothing but a lazy, drunken, fat slob, and furthermore . . ."

The man sighs and says, "It's started . . ."

My message to the troops is a simple one – THANK YOU!

Mark Salmon

Two blondes are on a plane, flying to California for the summer. They are about two hours into the flight when the pilot gets on the intercom and says, "We just lost an engine. It is all right we have three more, but it will take us an hour longer." Half an hour later he gets on the intercom again and says, "We just lost another engine. It's all right we have two more, it will take us another half hour though." One of the blondes turns to the other and says, "If we lose the two last engines we will be up here all day."

To all in the sandpit – come home safe!
Thinking of you always.

Angela Cheveley

What do you call a fly with no wings?
A walk!

**Thank you for our freedom.
We are very proud.**

Amy, 11, and Jessica, 7

Rodney was reading the morning newspaper when he came upon a study that said women use more words than men.

Excited to prove to his wife, Cathy, his long-held contention that women in general, and Cathy in particular, talked too much, he showed her the study results.

Rodney read the report to Cathy, "Men use about 15,000 words per day, but women use 30,000."

Cathy thought awhile, then finally she said to him, "It's because we have to repeat everything we say."

Rodney said, "What?"

Thinking of you and sending all our support.

Simone Drinkwater, Casemate

The RSM stormed into the CO's office and demanded leave.

"Look," protested the CO, "you've already had more than you're supposed to."

"Yeah, maybe so, but you don't know what I have to put up with," the RSM said, "Come with me."

Followed by the CO, he went out onto the parade ground and grabbed a new recruit. "Run over to my office and see if I'm there," he ordered.

Twenty minutes later the recruit returned, sweaty and out of breath.

"You're not there, sir," he reported.

"Oh, I see what you mean," conceded the CO, scratching his head. "I would have phoned."

Take care guys.
Thoughts are with you every day.

John Tindsley, Ex Army (22 years)

George Bush goes to a primary school to talk about the war. After his talk he offers question time. One little boy puts up his hand and George asks him what his name is. "Billy."

"And what is your question, Billy?"

Billy says, "I have three questions. First, why did the USA invade Iraq without the support of the UN? Second, why are you President when Al Gore got more votes? And third, whatever happened to Osama Bin Laden?"

Just then the bell rings for recess. George Bush informs the kiddies that they will continue after recess.

When they resume, George says, "OK, where were we? Oh that's right, question time. Who has a question?"

Another little boy puts up his hand. George points him out and asks him what his name is. "Steve."

"And what is your question, Steve?"

Steve says, "I have five questions. First, why did the USA invade Iraq without the support of the UN? Second, why are you President when Al Gore got more votes? Third, whatever happened to Osama Bin Laden? Fourth, why did the recess bell go off 20 minutes early? And fifth, what happened to Billy?"

You're making us all very proud back home.

Janet Dale

Two elderly friends were playing cards when one looked at the other and said, "Now don't get mad at me, I know we've been friends for a long time, but I just can't think of your name! I've thought and thought, but I can't remember it. Please tell me what your name is."
Her friend glared at her. For at least three minutes she just stared and glared at her. Finally she said, "How soon do you need to know?"

I am very proud to be British. We have the best Armed Forces in the world!

Jim Tierney

A woman walks into the store and purchases
the following:

1 small box of washing powder
1 Microwave meal for one
1 Bar of soap
3 individual servings of yoghurt
2 oranges
1 stick of women's deodorant.

She then goes to the till.
Cashier: Oh, you must be single
Woman: You can tell that by what I bought?
Cashier: No, you're ugly!

**To the men and women of our armed forces,
thank you for all that you do to keep us
safe!**

Deborah Milton

One day an American Indian boy asked his father why they have such long names.

The dad answers, "Well son, whenever a American Indian baby is born the father goes outside and names the baby after the first thing he sees . . . Why do you ask, Two Dogs Running?"

Be lucky!

Dave Partridge

Mr Johnson and his secretary are on a train to Paris.

They are just about to go to sleep when the secretary, who has the hots for her boss, says in a seductive voice, "I'm a little cold, could I borrow your blanket?"

The man says "How would you like to be Mrs. Johnson for a while?"

The secretary jumps at the chance and begins to get out of bed.

Then he adds, "Good, then you can get your own damn blanket."

Anon

One day a girl brings home her boyfriend and tells her father she wants to marry him. After talking to him for a while, he tells his daughter she can't marry him because he's her half-brother.

The same problem happens again four more times! The girl starts to get very fed up.

She goes to her mom and says, "Mum . . . what have you been doing all your life? Dad's been going around having children with women everywhere and now I can't marry any of the five guys I like because they have turned out to be my half-brothers!"

Her mum replies, "Don't worry darling, you can marry any one of them you want, he isn't really your dad."

Please let all our troops know how proud I am of them all and I wish them a safe time in Afghanistan.

Joanne David

A man went to apply for a job. After filling out all of his applications, he waited anxiously for the outcome. The employer read all his applications and said, "We have an opening for people like you." "Oh, great," he said, "what is it?"
"It's called the door!"

Laughter is the best medicine so I hope you get to laugh often! Keep safe.

Susan Mapping

A burglar breaks into a house. He sees a CD player that he wants, so he takes it.

Then he hears a voice, "Jesus is watching you."

He looks around with his flashlight wondering where the hell the voice was coming from.

He spots some money on a table and takes it.

Once again he hears a voice, "Jesus is watching you."

He hides in a corner trying to work out where the voice is coming from. He spots a birdcage with a parrot in it!

He goes over and asks, "Was that you?"

The parrot answered, "Yes."

The burglar then says, "What's your name?"

The parrot replies, "Moses."

The burglar says, "What kind of person names his bird Moses?"

The parrot replies, "THE SAME PERSON THAT NAMES HIS ROTTWEILER 'JESUS'."

With best wishes from an Ex-Squaddie.

John Barton

A cowboy rode into a new town and stopped at a saloon for a drink. Unfortunately, the locals had a habit of picking on strangers. When he finished his drink, he found his horse had been stolen. He went back into the bar, handily flipped his gun into the air, caught it above his head without even looking and fired a shot into the ceiling.

"Which one of you sidewinders stole my horse?!" he yelled with surprising forcefulness.

No one answered.

"Alright, I'm gonna have another beer, and if my horse ain't back outside by the time I finish, I'm gonna do what I dun in Texas! And I don't like to have to do what I dun in Texas!"

Some of the locals shifted restlessly.

The man, true to his word, had another beer, walked outside, and found his horse returned to the post. He saddled up and started to ride out of town. The bartender wandered out of the bar and asked, "Say partner, before you go . . . what happened in Texas?"

The cowboy turned back and said, "I had to walk home."

I served with the USMC and I'm real proud to have served with British troops!

Lance Davidson

Two lady dog owners are arguing about which of their dogs is smarter . . .

First Woman: "My dog is so clever, every morning he waits for the paper boy to come around and then he takes the newspaper and brings it to me."

Second Woman: "I know . . ."

First Woman: "How?"

Second Woman: "My dog told me."

Anon

While proudly showing off his new apartment to friends, a college student led the way into the den. "What is the big brass gong and hammer for?" one of his friends asked.
"That is the talking clock," the man replied.
"How does it work?"
"Watch," the man said and proceeded to give the gong an ear-shattering strike with the hammer. Suddenly, someone screamed from the other side of the wall, "Knock it off, you idiot! It's two o'clock in the morning!"

For all those who have served our country.

Roger Brackett

A young bride and groom-to-be had just
selected their wedding rings.
As the young lady admired the plain platinum
and diamond band she had chosen for
herself, she suddenly looked concerned.
"Tell me," she asked the rather elderly
salesman, "is there anything special I'll have
to do to take care of this ring?"
With a fatherly smile, the salesman said, "One
of the best ways to protect a wedding ring is
to soak it in dishwater."

Celer et audax. For all Riflemen.

Tom Shelby

What do you get when you cross a snowman with a vampire?
Frostbite.

Where do polar bears vote?
The North Poll

Where do snowmen keep their money?
In snow banks.

What's brown and sticky?
A stick.

Thank you for keeping us safe.

Jordan Jones, 10

A man was walking in the woods and came to a cottage where the walls were covered with clocks. He asked the woman who owned the cottage what all the clocks were for. She replied that everyone in the world had a clock, and every time you told a lie your clock advanced a second. He saw a clock that was hardly moving and when he remarked about it, he was told that it belonged to Mother Teresa. He then asked where Tony Blair's clock was. The woman replied, "It's in the kitchen, we're using it as a ceiling fan."

I hope this book gives you all a welcome lift when you need it most. Keep safe.

Anthony Barber

A librarian was woken up by the phone ringing.
"What time does the library open?" the man
on the phone asked.
"Nine a.m." came the reply. "And what's the
idea of calling me at home in the middle of
the night to ask a question like that?"
"Not until nine a.m.?" the man asked in a
disappointed voice.
"No, not till nine a.m.!" the librarian said.
"Why do you want to get in before nine A.M.?"
"Who said I wanted to get in?" the man
sighed sadly. "I want to get out."

**A sense of humour helped me a great deal.
Never lose yours. Stay safe.**

Lisa Collins

Steven Spielberg was busy discussing his new action adventure about famous classical composers. Bruce Willis, Sylvester Stallone and Arnold Schwarzenegger were in the room.

"Who do you want to play?" Spielberg asked Bruce Willis.

"I've always been a big fan of Chopin," said Bruce. "I'll play him."

"And you, Sylvester?" asked Spielberg.

"Mozart's the one for me!" said Sly.

"And what about you?" Spielberg asked Arnold Schwarzenegger.

"I'll be Bach," said Arnie.

**For anyone who has served in "the mob".
God bless you all.**

Mike Lewis

Two elderly couples were enjoying friendly conversation when one of the men asked the other, "Fred, how was the memory clinic you went to last month?"

"Outstanding!" Fred replied, "They taught us all the latest psychological techniques – visualization, association – it's made a big difference for me."

"That's great! What was the name of that clinic?" Fred went blank. He thought and thought but couldn't remember. Then a smile broke across his face and he asked, "What do you call that flower with the long stem and thorns?"

"You mean a rose?"

"Yes, that's it!" He turned to his wife. "Rose, what was the name of that clinic?"

Paul Gray

We've had so many "Doctor, Doctor" jokes that we thought we'd put them all together for you. Enjoy!

Doctor, Doctor, I swallowed a bone.
Are you choking?
No, I really did!

Doctor, Doctor, I think I need glasses.
You certainly do, Sir, this is a fish and chip shop!

Doctor, Doctor, my son has swallowed my pen, what should I do?
Use a pencil until I get there.

Doctor, Doctor, I think I'm a bell.
Take these and if it doesn't help give me a ring!

Doctor, Doctor, I think I'm suffering from deja vu!
Didn't I see you yesterday?

Doctor, Doctor, I've got wind! Can you give
me something?
Yes – here's a kite!

Doctor, Doctor, how do I stop my nose from
running?!
Stick your foot out and trip it up!

Doctor, Doctor, I tend to flush a lot.
Don't worry it's just a chain reaction!

Doctor, Doctor, I keep thinking I'm a bee.
Buzz off, can't you see I'm busy?

Doctor, Doctor, these pills you gave me
for BO . . .
What's wrong with them?
They keep slipping out from under my arms!

Doctor, Doctor, everyone keeps throwing me
in the garbage.
Don't talk rubbish!

Doctor, Doctor, I feel like a sheep.
That's baaaaaaaaaad!

Doctor, Doctor, I keep getting pains in the eye
when I drink coffee.
Have you tried taking the spoon out?

Doctor, Doctor, I feel like a spoon!
Well sit still and don't stir!

Doctor, Doctor, I feel like a pack of cards.
I'll deal with you later.

Doctor, Doctor, have you got something for a
bad headache?
Of course. Just take this
hammer and hit yourself in
the head. Then you'll have a
bad headache.

Doctor, Doctor, I keep
thinking there is two of
me.
One at a time please.

After two weeks of basic training, a sergeant lined up his new recruits and asked them each who they would like to spend an hour with if given the chance right now. Several soldiers answered their mothers, their girlfriends, etc. Then the sergeant heard a unique answer.

Sergeant: "Private, who would you most like to be alone with for an hour?"

Private: "My careers advisor, Sarge!"

From an old one to many others. Heads down and stay safe.

Richard Jenkins

On a street corner in London:
A gentleman walked up to a soldier
and asked, "Pardon me, sir, which
side is the MOD on?"
"Ours, mostly."

Be proud, we are!

Bob Hamilton

The ship navigator fell sick when the ship was far out to sea. The doctor examined the navigator and then thought deeply for a long time.

"What's up, Doc," asked the sick man, "can't decide what medicine to prescribe me?"

"No, I'm trying to remember who, except you, knows anything about navigation here."

Anon

Officer: "Soldier, do you have change for a pound?"

Soldier: "Yes, mate, of course."

Officer: "That's no way to address an officer! Now let's try it again. Do you have change for a pound?"

Soldier: "No, SIR!"

Having served many years ago I know the importance of a good laugh. Chins up and at 'em!

Graham Billington

During training exercises, the lieutenant who was driving down a muddy back road encountered another car stuck in the mud with a red-faced colonel at the wheel. "Your jeep stuck, sir?" asked the lieutenant as he pulled alongside. "Nope," replied the colonel, coming over and handing him the keys, "Yours is."

My husband, an ex-lieutenant in the Royal Green Jackets told me this many years ago. It still makes me smile today. I hope it will brighten your days too.

Mary Bourne

The Company Commander and the RSM were in the field. As they hit the sack for the night, the RSM said, "Sir, look up into the sky and tell me what you see?"

The CO said, "I see millions of stars."

RSM: "And what does that tell you, sir?"

CO: "Astronomically, it tells me that there are millions of galaxies and potentially billions of planets. Theologically, it tells me that God is great and that we are small and insignificant. Meteorologically, it tells me that we will have a beautiful day tomorrow. What does it tell you?"

RSM: "Well sir, it tells me that somebody stole our tent."

Overwhelmed by the efforts you are going to out there. Stay safe!

Brian Spellman

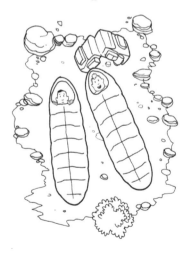

A guy was telling his mate about this girl, Sue, who disguised herself as a man and joined the army. "But, wait a minute," said his friend, "She'd have to dress with the boys and shower with them, too, won't she?"
"Sure," replied the guy.
"Well, won't they find out?"
The guy shrugged. "Who's gonna tell?"

Keep safe.

Jenny Davis

How do you know if there is an
RAF fighter pilot at your party?
He'll tell you.

What's the difference between God
and RAF fighter pilots?
God doesn't think he's an RAF
fighter pilot.

What's the difference between an
RAF fighter pilot and a jet engine?
A jet engine stops whining when
the plane shuts down.

Anon
(although we suspect it may be ground crew . . .)

Having passed the physical, Jon was asked by the doctor, "Why do you want to join the Navy, son?" "My father said it'd be a good idea, sir."
"Oh? And what does your father do?"
"He's in the Army, sir."

Thoughts are with you all.

Alan Winters

Two 80-year-old men are driving down the road when they hear the Ex-Lax commercial end with the statement: "It makes you feel young again."

John looks at Sylvester and says, "We need to pull over and get a bottle of that stuff!"

Sylvester agrees and the two old men pull over and get a bottle of Ex-Lax. They both take two tablespoons each and continue to drive.

About one mile later Sylvester asks, "Well John, do you feel young yet?"

"No," replies John.

So they pull over and take four more tablespoons apiece and continue to drive down the road.

A couple of miles later, Sylvester asks, "John, do you feel younger?"

"No," replies John, "but I did a very childish thing!"

Chris Walsh

A captain on his ship was disturbed by his assistant telling him, "Sir! Sir! There are five enemy ships on the horizon."
The captain tells the man, "Get my red coat and prepare for battle!"
The assistant runs without question to get the captain's red coat and prepares for battle.
After their victory the assistant asks the captain why he wanted his red coat.
The captain tells the assistant, "If I was shot, you would not have been able to tell I was bleeding, and you would keep fighting."
The assistant was really impressed.
The next day the assistant came to the captain, "Sir! Sir! There are twenty enemy ships on the horizon!"
The captain was stunned. He looked at the assistant and told him, "Get me my brown pants!"

You put the GREAT into Great Britain! Stay safe.

Mark Jarvis

What's red and sits in the corner?
A naughty bus!

Anon.

A senior citizen picked up his brand new Porsche convertible and drove out of the car dealership. As he is going down the road, he decides to floor it up to 80 mph, enjoying the wind passing through the little hair he had.

"Amazing," he felt as he flew down the dual carriageway. He jams the pedal down even more as he looks in his rear-view mirror and sees a police car right behind him, lights a-flashing and siren a-blaring.

So he floored it to 100 mph, then 110, then 120 ... suddenly he thought, "What am I doing, I'm too old for this!" and pulls over to await the policeman's arrival.

The policeman pulls in behind him, walks up to the Porsche, looks at his watch and says, "Sir, my shift ends in 30 minutes. Today is Friday. If you can give me one good reason for your speeding that I've never heard of before, I'll let you go on your way."

Well the senior citizen paused. Then he explained that, "Years ago, my wife ran off with a policeman and I thought you were bringing her back to me!"

"Very well! Have a good day, sir," replied the policeman.

Best wishes and thanks to you all!

Michael Davidson

Fred got home from his Sunday round of golf later than normal and very tired.

"Bad day at the course?" his wife asked.

"Everything was going fine," he said. "Then Harry had a heart attack and died on the 10th tee."

"Oh, that's awful!"

"You're not kidding. For the whole back nine it was hit the ball, drag Harry, hit the ball, drag Harry."

Keep safe!

Bill Morris

A blonde woman walks into a hardware store and asks for a chain saw that will cut six trees in one hour.

The salesman recommends the top of the line model. The woman is suitably impressed, and buys it.

The next day she brings it back and says, "This chainsaw is defective. It would only cut down one tree and it took ALL DAMN DAY!"

The salesman takes the chain saw, starts it up to see what's wrong, and the woman shouts, "What's that noise?"

Thank you for keeping us safe and free!

Jane Matthew

Deep within a forest, a little turtle began to climb a tree. After hours of effort he reached the top, jumped into the air waving his front legs and crashed to the ground. After recovering, he slowly climbed the tree again, jumped, and fell to the ground.

The turtle tried again and again while a couple of birds sitting on a branch watched his sad efforts.

Finally, the female bird turned to her mate. "Dear," she chirped, "I think it's time to tell him he's adopted."

With my sincerest and proudest thanks to you all. I am forever grateful for your sacrifice and service.

David Trimming

One day, as a dog was walking by a store, he noticed a sign which said, "Now Hiring: must be able to type 70 words per minute, and must be bilingual. Equal opportunity employment."

The dog took the sign in his mouth and brought it into the manager's office. He set it down on the desk. When the manager realized that the dog was applying for the job, he laughed and said, "I'm not going to hire a dog!"

The dog put his paw on the part of the sign that read "equal opportunity employer."

"Well," said the manager, "let's see you type 70 words per minute!" He handed the dog a document and watched as the dog perfectly duplicated the document, and well over 70 words per minute. The man looked at the dog. He couldn't believe it.

"Don't tell me you're bilingual too."

The dog opened his mouth and said, "Meow."

I hope this brings a smile when it's most needed.

Phillip Potter

Three girls walk into a bar; a brunette, a redhead and a green-haired girl. The bartender asks the brunette how she keeps her hair so brown.
The brunette combs her hands through her hair and says, "It's natural, it's natural."
Then the bartender asks the redhead how she keeps her hair so red. She combs her hands through her hair and says, "It's natural, it's natural."
Then he asks the green-haired girl how she keeps her hair so green. She sneezes into her hands, combs her hands through her hair and says, "It's natural, it's natural."

Please come home safe but know how proud we all are of you.

Susan Mills

Q: How many psychiatrists does it take to change a light bulb?
A: Only one, but the light bulb has to WANT to change.

The sacrifices of those who have served in our armed forces must never be forgotten. I am proud to say I am British and I have served in our forces. Utrinque Paratus!

P. Owens

Q: What do you call a man with no legs?

A: Doesn't matter, he's not coming!

Sending my best wishes to everyone serving around the world at Christmas time. Come home safely.

S. Samson

A 55-year-old man decides he needs to get into shape. He visits the gym, where a trainer asks him if he could do the splits. "Of course I can't." he answers. "How flexible are you?" she asks. To which he replies, "Well, I can't do Thursdays."

Faithful in adversity. Keep safe and keep laughing!

Mike Gooch

Did you hear of the soldier who was subjected to mustard gas and pepper spray and didn't bat an eyelid?
He was a seasoned veteran...

From an old soldier, stay safe boys.

"How many people work in your office?" the boss asked the department head.
"Oh, about half of them, sir!"

My father served in the RAF and I am forever grateful and full of respect for anyone who serves our country! Come home safe.

Gloria Simmonds

A little girl asked her mother, "How did the human race appear?" The mother answered, "God made Adam and Eve and they had children and so was all mankind made." Two days later, the girl asked her father the same question. The father answered, "Many years ago there were monkeys from which the human race evolved."
The confused girl returned to her mother and said, "Mom, how is it possible that you told me the human race was created by God, and Dad said they developed from monkeys?" The mother answered, "Well, dear, it is very simple. I told you about my side of the family and your father told you about his."

For all who have served our country – THANK YOU!

Mrs M. Collins

"The car won't start," said a wife to her husband, "I think there's water in the carburettor."

"How do you know?" said the husband scornfully, "You don't even know what the carburettor is."

"I'm telling you," repeated the wife, "I'm sure there's water in the carburettor."

"We'll see," mocked the husband, "Let me check it out. Where's the car?"

"In the swimming pool."

D. Johnson

Two elderly women were discussing their husbands over tea.
"I do wish that my husband would stop biting his nails. He makes me terribly nervous."
"Mine used to do the same thing," the older woman replied. "But I broke him of the habit."
"How?"
"I hid his teeth."

I cannot imagine what it's like to fight in a war but I am very proud that you all do to keep us safe. Thank you.

Melanie Smith

A Polish student was in his college campus bookstore.
Questioning the store clerk about a book for one of his classes, the clerk responded, "This book will do half the job for you."
"Good," the Polack replied, "I'll take two."

My father fought in World War II and I have grown up with maximum respect for the British Armed Forces. I am now very proud to live in the UK. Keep well and safely.

Marius Waricki

Give a man a fish and you feed him for a day.
Teach him to use the Internet, and he won't bother you for weeks!

With love to you all from an ex-Army wife. Please stay safe and happy.

Maria Jarvis

The MoD have announced today that after carrying out tests in Cumbria, they are to scrap the Snatch Land Rover for something which provides its occupants with a better fire position, so have put in an order for 500 Citroen Picassos.

Thank you

G. Rossal

A skeleton walks into a bar and orders a beer and a mop.

My thoughts are with you all every day. Keep safe.

Gary English

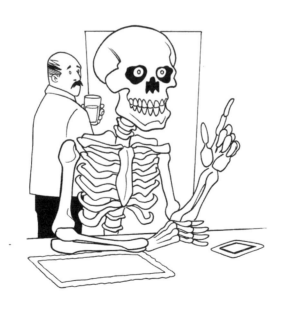

If it's true that girls are inclined to marry men like their fathers, it is understandable why so many mothers cry so much at weddings.

Maximum respect to you all.

Gill Davy

Two lawyers walking through the woods spot a vicious-looking bear. The first lawyer immediately opens his briefcase, pulls out a pair of trainers and starts putting them on. The second lawyer looks at him and says, "You're crazy! You'll never be able to outrun that bear!" "I don't have to," the first lawyer replies, "I only have to outrun you."

We're all thinking of you and hope you have a good one wherever you are!

E. Maulings

A lawyer was on his deathbed in his bedroom, and he called to his wife.

She rushed in and said, "What is it, honey?"

He told her to run and get the bible as soon as possible.

Being a religious woman, she thought this was a good idea. She ran and got it, preparing to read him his favourite verse or something of the sort. He snatched it from her and quickly began scanning pages, his eyes darting right and left.

The wife was curious, so she asked, "What are you doing, honey?"

"I'm looking for loopholes!" he shouted.

Thank you all for what you do :)

Lucy and Steve

A dentist, a nurse and an army general are flying. The dentist decides to drop a tooth brush out of the plane. The nurse drops down a medical kit and the army general drops a bomb. They land the airplane and see what happened...

First, they found a guy looking for his false teeth.

Next, they found a guy bandaging his wounds.

Lastly, they found a young boy laughing his head off.

They asked him what happened and he said, "My grandfather farted and blew up his house."

I'm so glad we have you guys and galls to protect us at night.

Pete Taylor

A police recruit was asked during the exam, "What would you do if you had to arrest your own mother?"
He answered, "Call for backup."

Thinking of you all and hope you all come home safe.

Anon

A priest and a nun are golfing, and the priest is up. He swings, misses and exclaims, "Oh My God, I missed!"
The nun gives him a dirty look, but he swings again, misses and exclaims, "Oh My God, I missed!"
The nun stares at him and says, "If you say that one more time, God will open up the heavens and strike you with a lightning bolt!"
So, the priest swings again and exclaims "Oh My God, I ....missed!"
Suddenly, a lightning bolt shoots out of the sky and strikes the nun. All that is heard in the sky is, "Oh My God, I missed."

Stay safe and come home soon.

E. Jones

A man in a hot air balloon, realising he was lost, reduced altitude and spotted a woman below. He descended further and shouted to the lady, "Excuse me, can you help me? I promised a friend I would meet him an hour ago but I don't know where I am."

The woman below replied, "You're in a hot air balloon, hovering approximately 30 feet above the ground. You're between 40 and 41 degrees north latitude and between 59 and 60 degrees west longitude."

"You must work with computers," said the balloonist.

"Actually I do," replied the woman, "How did you know?"

"Well," answered the balloonist, "everything you have told me is technically correct but I've no idea what to make of your information and the fact is I'm still lost.

Frankly, you've been as helpful as a chocolate teapot. If anything, you've delayed my trip."
The woman below responded, "You must be an Army Officer."
"I am," replied the balloonist, "but how did you know?"
"Well," said the woman, "you don't know where you are or where you're going. You have risen to where you are due to a large quantity of hot air. You made a promise, which you've no idea how to keep and you expect people beneath you to solve your problems. The fact is you are in exactly the same position you were in before we met but now, somehow, it's my fault!"

We are forever in your debt, thank you.

A. Porrit

A new pastor was visiting the homes of his parishioners.

At one house it seemed obvious that someone was at home, but no answer came to his repeated knocks at the door. Therefore, he took out a card and wrote, "Revelation 3:20" on the back of it and stuck it in the door.

When the offering was processed the following Sunday, he found that his card had been returned. Added to it was this cryptic message, "Genesis 3:10."

Reaching for his Bible to check out the citation, he broke up in gales of laughter. Revelation 3:20 begins, "Behold, I stand at the door and knock."

Genesis 3:10 reads, "I heard your voice in the garden and I was afraid, for I was naked."

Love and hugs to you all.

Suzy

There was a family which had a parrot that was always embarrassing them with its bad language. So one day, the boy took the parrot and stuck him in the freezer. Two hours later the squawking stopped.

The kid checked the freezer and the parrot said, "Okay I'll stop cussing, but I have one question."

The boy said, "What?"

The parrot asked, "What did the turkey do?"

Merry Christmas.

R. Dier

A little boy asked his father, "Daddy, how much does it cost to get married?"
The father replied, "I don't know, son, I'm still paying for it."

Praying for you all.

H. Jules

A priest was preparing a man for his long journey into the night. Whispering firmly, the priest said, "Denounce the devil! Let him know how little you think of his evil." The dying man said nothing. The priest repeated his order. Still, the dying man said nothing. The priest asked, "Why do you refuse to denounce the devil and his evil?" The dying man said, "Until I know where I'm heading, I don't think I ought to aggravate anybody."

Big hugs to you all lads.

Liz

There was once three fish (mom, dad, son)
who needed a place to sleep.
The mom slept in the kitchen sink.
The dad slept in the bathtub.
The son slept in the toilet.
The next morning, the dad asked the mom
how her night was.
"Okay, but it was a little too small," said the
mom.
The mom asked the dad how his night was.
"Just fine. There was a lot of room to swim,"
said the dad.
The dad asked his son how his night was.
"Horrible!" said the son. "It was raining scat
and logs all night long!"

Chin up lads, you'll be home soon x

Y. Fuller

If Life Was Like A Computer:
You could add/remove someone in your life using the control panel.
You could put your kids in the recycle bin and restore them when you feel like it!
You could improve your appearance by adjusting the display settings.
You could turn off the speakers when life gets too noisy.
You could click on "find" to recover your lost remote control and car keys.
To get your daily exercise, just click on "run"!
If you mess up your life, you could always press "Ctrl, Alt, Delete" and start all over!

Go get 'em lads!

Anon

A middle-aged woman has a heart attack and is taken to the hospital. While on the operating table she has a near-death experience. During that experience she sees God and asks if this is it. God says no and explains that she has another 30 years to live. Upon her recovery, she decides to just stay in the hospital and have a face lift, liposuction, breast augmentation, tummy tuck, etc. She even has someone come in and change her hair colour. She figures that since she's got another 30 years, she might as well make the most of it.

She walks out of the hospital after the last operation and is killed by an ambulance speeding by. She arrives in front of God and complains, "I thought you said I had another 30 years!"

God replies, "I didn't recognize you!"

You guys rock!!!

Dave and the lads

Three women are at a house, one redhead, one brunette, and one blonde.
A genie appears and says the women can say anything, but if they tell a lie, they will disappear.
The redhead says, "I think I am the smartest woman ever," and she disappears.
The brunette says, "I think I am the most beautiful woman on Earth," and she disappears.
The blonde says, "I think –" and she disappears.

Hopes this cheers you up a bit till you can get home to your loved ones.

F. White

One day, the Prime Minister fell off a bridge and was saved by three young boys. The Prime Minister thanked them and said he'd give them all one thing in the whole world. The first boy asked for a trip to Disneyland and *voila!* that summer he was in Disneyland. The second boy asked for a pair of Nike Shocks and sure enough, the next day he was wearing a pair of trainers. The third boy asked for a wheelchair with a plasma TV, cup holders and hydraulics. The Prime Minister, looking puzzled at the boy, asked why he wanted a wheelchair because he didn't look disabled. The young boy replied, "I will be after my father finds out that I saved you!"

We're so lucky as a family that we're safe, and it's all down to you boys (and girls), thank you.

Andy, Shelly, and Danny

Q: How do you play Taliban bingo?
A: B-52... F-16... B-1...

Q: What is the Taliban's national bird?
A: Duck

Q: What's the five-day forecast for Afghanistan?
A: Two days

Thank you guys, top show.

Tarquin

A businessman on his deathbed called his friend and said, "Bill, I want you to promise me that when I die, you will have my remains cremated." "And what," his friend asked, "do you want me to do with your ashes?" The businessman said, "Just put them in an envelope and post them to the Inland Revenue. Include a note that says, "Now, you have everything."

Keep your heads down and come home soon to your loved ones.

F. Willets

A woman went on a tour of the White House. As the guide led her down one of the historic halls, a door burst open and a large aquatic sea mammal, balancing a beach ball on its nose, scurried past.

"My, what was that?" exclaimed the woman.

"Oh, that's just the Presidential Seal," replied the guide.

We're all rooting for you, do your best but please stay safe.

Anon

There were 3 construction workers who always got the same thing for lunch. All of them were tired of eating the same thing over and over again.

1st worker: "I hate sandwiches, if I get sandwiches for lunch again tomorrow, I'm jumping off that bridge."

2nd worker: "Oh my Gosh! If I see another taco I'm going to jump off that bridge tomorrow."

3rd worker: "Beans AGAIN?!! I will jump off that bridge tomorrow if I get beans for lunch tomorrow."

The next day they all got the same thing for lunch so each jumped off the bridge and died. Their wives were inconsolable.

1st wife: "If I knew he would do that I would have never packed him sandwiches!"

2nd wife: "If I knew he would do that, I would have never packed him tacos!"

3rd wife: "If I knew he would do that, I never would have let him pack his own lunch!"

Can't stop thinking of you all out there, please come home – we miss you all.

Terry

What is the most dangerous thing you can eat?
Wedding cake!

Forever grateful for what you do!

Jack Williams

A man was walking along the beach when he found an ancient bottle. When he rubbed the bottle, a genie appeared. The genie told him that he would grant him 3 wishes, but that his mother-in-law would get twice as much as he asked for.

"What's with that?" the man asked. "That's the way it has to be," answered the genie.

So the man said, "OK, give me a million dollars".

"Fine," said the genie. He gave the man a million dollars and the mother-in-law received 2 million dollars.

Seeing how this was going, the man said, "OK, give me a big house with a pool, tennis court, bowling alley, movie theatre and a Bentley in the garage."

The genie said, "It's done," and the mother-in-law received 2 of the same.

Then the genie said, " OK, that's two wishes, what's the last one?"

"OK, then why don't you just beat me half to death!"

Hope you have a good Christmas, troops (and veterans).

Heather and Steve Bailey

A man goes to the doctor's and says, "Doctor, I've known you a long time and I hope you understand my sensitive problem." "Of course," says the doctor, "what's the problem?" The man replies, "I think I'm a moth." "Oh," says the doctor, "well you really need to see our psychiatrist." "I am," says the man, "but I saw your light on and had to come in!"

I couldn't do what you lot do, but I will always support you!

V. Mine

Preparation For Leaving The Armed Forces . . .
This guide will assist you in your efforts to "Fit In" with civilians when you leave the forces.

1. I am in the military, I have a problem.
This is the first step to recovery . . .

2. Speech:
Time should never begin with a zero or end in a hundred, it is not 0530 or 1400 it is 5:30 in the morning (AKA God-awful early).
Words like deck, rack, and "PT" will get you weird looks: floor, bed, workout, get used to it.
"Fuck" cannot be used to replace whatever word you can't think of right now, try "um".
Grunting is not talking.
It's a phone, not a radio, conversations on a phone do not end in "out".
People will not know what you are talking about if you tell them you are coming from Dalton Bks with the CP platoon or that you spent a deployment with the HAC.

3. Style:
Do not put creases in your jeans.
Do not put creases on the front of your dress shirts.
A horseshoe cut looks dumb, not motivating.
A high and tight looks really dumb as well.
So does a low reg, but not as bad.
A hat indoors does not make you a bad person, it makes you like the rest of the world.
You do not have to wear a belt ALL the time.

4. Women:
Air Force girls are easy, very easy, not all women are this easy and will probably punch you in the nuts if you treat them like Air Force girls.
Being divorced twice by the time you are 23 is not normal, neither are six-month marriages, even if it is your first.
Marrying a girl so that you can move out of the barracks does not make "financial sense", it makes you a retard.

5. Personal accomplishments:
In the real world, being able to do push-ups will not make you good at your job.
Most people will be slightly disturbed by you if you tell them about people you have killed or seen die.
How much pain you can take is not a personal accomplishment.
The time you got really drunk and passed the sobriety test anyway is also not a personal accomplishment.

6. Drinking:
In the real world, being drunk before 5p.m. will get you a written warning, not a "good for you".
That time you drank a 5th of Jaeger and pissed in your closet is not a conversation starter.
That time you went to the combat life-saver school and practiced giving vodka IVs will also not be a good conversation starter.

7. Bodily functions:
Farting on your co-workers and then giggling while you run away may be viewed as "unprofessional".
The size of the dump you took yesterday will not be funny no matter how big it was, how much it burned, or how

much it smelled.

You can't make fun of someone for being sick, no matter how funny it is.

VD will also not be funny.

8. The human body:

Most people will not want to hear about your balls. Odd as that may seem, it's true.

9. Spending habits:

One day, you will have to pay bills.

Buying a £30,000 car on a £16,000 a year salary is a really bad idea.

Spending money on video games instead of on nappies makes you a fool.

One day you will need health insurance.

10. Interacting with civilians (AKA you):

Making fun of your neighbour to his face for being fat will not be normal.

11. Real jobs:

They really can fire you.

On the flip side you really can quit.

Screaming at the people who work for you will not be normal, remember they really can quit too.

Taking naps at work will not be acceptable.

Remember 9–5 not 0530 to 1800.

12. The law:

Non-judicial punishment does not exist and will not save you from prison.

Your workplace unlike your command can't save you and

probably won't, in fact most likely you will fired about five minutes after they find out you've been arrested.

Even McDonalds does background checks, and "conviction" isn't going to help you get the job.

Fighting is not a normal thing and will get you really arrested, not yelled at Monday morning before they ask you if you won.

13. General knowledge:

You can in fact really say what you think about the Queen in public.

Pain is not weakness leaving the body, it's just pain.

They won't wear anything shiny that tells you they are more important then you are, be polite.

Read the contracts before you sign them, remember what happened the first time.

You have all shown the world the true, true meaning of "Selfless Commitment, Courage, Discipline, Integrity, Loyalty and Respect for Others." Your individual courage is something the United Kingdom is very proud of. Thank you from the bottom of my heart for being the "True Heroes" that you all are. Take care, stay safe and keep "Smiling" always!

Anita Taylor

A woman was taking golf lessons, and she had started her first round when she was stung by a bee. She went back into the clubhouse for help. Her golf teacher asked why she was back in so early, so she told him of the bee sting. "Where did it sting you?" he asked. "Between the 1st and 2nd hole." He shook his head and said, "Then you had your feet too far apart!"

John Marable, Ex Army Sgt of 22 years

I was on my way to work the other morning and took a shortcut through the cemetery. I noticed a guy crouched down behind a headstone so I said, "Morning!" and he said, "No, just taking a dump."

Keep up the good work guys, I'm proud of you all.

Steve Jones

Veronica had just split up with her fiancé and decided she needed cheering up, so books into a top hotel for a weekend of total indulgence. Looking gorgeous, she takes the lift down to the cocktail bar and scans the room before sashaying up to the bar. Provocatively, she stands next to a handsome hunk who's sitting on a bar stool, idly playing with his very unusual-looking watch. She is about to order a drink when she feels the urge to speak:

"Ooooh, that's a very posh-looking watch." she says.

"Why thank you, young lady. Actually it'sh quite shpeshul. Ah – forgive me . . . may I offer you a drink; the namesh Bond, by the way, Jamesh Bond."

"Why thank you, James, I'm Veronica; pleased to meet you. What would you recommend?"

"Barman: two Vodka Martinish, pleash, shaken, not shturred."

"So, James, what's so special about your watch?"

"Well, it ushesh alpha wavesh and delta wavesh to ashesh what people are thinking."

"It must have been FRIGHTFULLY expensive to develop!" she exclaims.

"Sheveral hundred thoushand poundsh."

"Goodness! Well, for all that money, I hope it does a little more than tell the time and fiddle with some waves?"

"Actually, it can alsho tell what shum people have on their bodiesh . . ." explains Bond.

"Ooh!" says Veronica, "what's it telling you now?"

"Well, thish ish a wee bit delicate, but it shaysh you're not wearing any pantiesh . . ."

She blushes a little, giggles and replies, "All that money, James, but I'm afraid it's wrong: I am wearing panties!"
Bond looks down, taps his watch a couple of times then holds it to his ear and says "Bloody thing'sh running an hour fasht!"

As one who has served before, I know that you honour our nation with your service. I can only hope that – one day – the nation will honour your service in return.

Mike Chirnside, Ex-Royal Navy

A guy walks into his house and into the lounge where his wife is sitting alone. He is carrying a duck under his arm.

He says, "This is the pig I've been shagging for the past 15 years."

His wife looks up and says, "That's not a pig!"

The husband says, "I wasn't fucking talking to you!"

Keep your heads down and your spirits up and come home safe.

Brian Harman

What was the first thing that Adam said to Eve?
"Stand back, I don't know how big this thing gets!"

Niamh Whelan

You're Taliban if . . .
You refine heroin for a living but have a moral
objection to beer.
You own a 3,000 quid machine gun and a 5,000 quid
rocket launcher but can't afford shoes.
You have more wives than teeth.
You think vests come in two styles: bulletproof and
suicide.
You can't think of anyone you HAVEN'T declared
jihad against.
Consider TV dangerous but routinely carry explosives
in your clothing.
You were amused to discover that mobile phones
have uses other than the setting of roadside bombs.
You've often uttered the phrase, "I love what you've
done with your cave."
You have nothing against women and think all men
should own at least one.
You bathe monthly whether necessary or not.
Or you've had a crush on your neighbour's goat!

**Hope this gave you some amusement. Keep at
it guys, you're doing a brilliant job out
there. Keep safe and when you come back,
treat yourself to a beer or five :)**

Connor Stuart

Ten Paras turn up at the Pearly Gates.
St Peter says, "Sorry guys, only enough room
for three, sort it out between yourselves
who's coming in."
St Peter heads for the NAAFI. Shortly after,
Angel Gabriel phones him and says,
"They've gone Peter."
"What, all ten of them?"
"No, the fuckin' GATES."

UTRINQUE PARATUS.

Charlie Marsden

I started reading Harry Potter but I think it's a bit far-fetched. I can buy into the fact that magic exists, and that there could be such things as unicorns and wizards . . . but a ginger bloke with two mates – No fucking way!

Bless all the lads 'n lasses who are put in harm's way. My respect, my thanks. Both my and my family's love go out to all of you. Stay safe, stay proud, give them hell. Pat-R.M.

Alan Patterson

A man goes to a doctor's surgery to get his wife's blood test results. The receptionist looks at him rather sheepishly and says, "I'm sorry Mr Jones but there is a slight problem. On the day your wife came in, another Mrs Jones did too and we have mixed up the results. One has AIDS and the other has Alzheimer's."

"So what the hell do we do now?" asks the man.

"Well," said the receptionist, "the doctor suggests you drop her off in town and if she finds her way home don't fuck her!'"

All our forces serving in Afghanistan make us very proud. They put the 'G' in Great Britain. Your country salutes you! We are not afraid to walk in the valley of the shadow of death for we are the British and we fear no evil!

John Shonfield, Ex-R Signals Gulf War 1

A woman is enjoying a relaxing bath when her four-year-old son walks in and asks, "Mummy, what's that between your legs?" Somewhat embarrassed and desperately thinking of an answer she blurts out, "Oh, that's where Daddy accidentally hit me with an axe!"
"Good shot! Right in the fanny!" replied the boy.

Danny Greeno

Paddy calls Easyjet to book a flight. The operator asks, "How many people are flying with you?" Paddy replies, "I don't know! It's your fucking plane!"

So proud, so grateful!

Sheila James

A young cowboy sitting in a saloon one Saturday night recognized an elderly man standing at the bar who, in his day, had been the fastest gun in the West. The cowboy took a place next to the old-timer, bought him a drink and told him of his great ambition to be a great shot . . .

"Could you give me some tips?" he asked.

The old man said, "Well, for one thing, you're wearing your gun too high – tie the holster a little lower down on your leg."

"Will that make me a better gunfighter?"

"Sure will!"

The young man did as he was told, stood up, whipped out his .44 and shot the bow tie off the piano player.

"That's terrific!" said the cowboy. "Got any more tips?"

"Yep," said the old man, "cut a notch out of your holster where the hammer hits it – that'll give you a smoother draw."

"Will that make me a better gunfighter?" asked the young man.

"You bet it will," said the old-timer.

The young man took out his knife, cut the notch, stood up, drew his gun in a blur, and then shot a cufflink off the piano player.

"Wow!" exclaimed the cowboy "I'm learnin' somethin' here. Got any more tips?"

The old man pointed to a large can in a corner of the saloon. "See that axle grease over there? Coat your gun with it."

The young man smeared some of the grease on the barrel of his gun.

"No," said the old-timer, "I mean smear it all over the gun, handle and all."

"Will that make me a better gunfighter?" asked the young man.

"No," said the old-timer, "but when Wyatt Earp gets done playing the piano, he's gonna shove that gun up your ass, and it won't hurt as much coated in grease."

My thoughts are with you all.

Michael Massy-Beresford, Ex-Oxf and Bucks

A 73-year-old woman in court for streaking at the Chelsea Flower Show . . . she was let off with a caution, but was awarded 1st prize for best dried arrangement.

Amandeep Uppal

A Rifleman was stood before his RSM requesting for special leave from overseas.

RSM: "Why do you want leave soldier."

RFN: "Well sir, my wife is in another unit back in the UK sir, and she's just been promoted to RSM."

RSM: "So why do you want special leave?"

RFN: "So I can fulfill a lifelong ambition sir."

Matthew Foulkes-Williams

I was walking along the other day when I found a lamp. I rubbed it and out pops a genie.

"One wish!" he says.

"Easy," says I, "I wish to live forever."

"No can do," says the genie, "I can't grant eternal life – it's against the rules."

"No problem," says I, "I wish to live long enough to see England win the World Cup."

"You sneaky bastard!" says the genie.

Alan Patterson

A priest is walking down the road when he comes across a young boy carrying a bottle of nitric acid. The priest thinks that this is a pretty dangerous item for a young boy to have.

The priest asks the young boy, "Is that a bottle of nitric acid you are carrying my son?"

The lad replies, "Yeah it is, why?"

The priest thinks hard for a minute and says, "I tell you what, I will swap you that bottle of nitric acid for a bottle of my holy water!"

"Why, what can your holy water do that my nitric acid can't?" asks the boy. "Well, if you rub some of my holy water onto a woman's stomach, she will pass a baby!"

"That's nothing," replies the lad, "if I rub this nitric acid onto a dog's bollocks, it'll pass a fucking motorbike!"

Very proud!

Anthony Behan, Ex 7 RHA

A man walks into a library and asks for a book on suicide. "Fuck off!" says the librarian, "you won't bring it back!"

Mark Ormrod, Former RM

Two nuns are driving along a country road when all of a sudden the devil appears on the bonnet. The novice in the passenger seat winds down her window, leans out and says, "Go away, go away you evil horror!"
The devil simply dances wildly and raises a finger to the shocked and terrified nun.
She turns in desperation to the mother superior who is driving and asks for advice.
Clutching her St Christopher necklace, she says "Have faith and show him your cross my dear, show him your cross."
The novice leans out of the window once more and shouts "FUCK OFF!"

Eternally proud of you all.

Steve Hutchinson

A virile, middle-aged Italian gentlemen named Guido was relaxing at his favourite bar in Rome when he managed to attract a spectacular young blonde woman.

Things progressed to the point where he invited her back to his apartment and, after some small talk, they retired to his bedroom where he rattled her senseless.

After a pleasant interlude he asked with a smile, "So, you finish?"

She paused for a second, frowned, and replied, "No."

Surprised, Guido reached for her and the rattling resumed.

This time she thrashed about wildly and there were screams of passion . . .

The sex finally ends and again, Guido smiles and asks, "You finish?"

Again, after a short pause, she returns his smile, cuddles closer to him and softly says, "No."

Stunned, but damned if he was going to leave this woman unsatisfied, Guido reaches for the woman yet again. Using the last of his strength, he barely manages it, but they end together screaming, bucking, clawing and ripping the bed sheets.

Exhausted, Guido falls onto his back, gasping. Barely able to turn his head, he looks into her eyes, smiles proudly and asked again,

"You finish?"

Barely able to speak, the beautiful blonde whispers in his ear,

"No, I Norwegian."

Lee Dodson

An old couple who have been friends in their care home for many years decide one day to have a crack at making love. The man, keen to do well, asks what she prefers. She says she likes oral sex and so the man sets to work. After a few seconds, however, the man sits up and says, "I'm sorry love but the smell is just too bad."

After thinking for a moment, the woman says it must be her arthritis that's caused the smell.

"Does arthritis make you smell like that?" asked the surprised man.

"No," replies the woman, "but it means I can't wipe my arse properly!"

Mark Timpson

God is feeling tired and decides to take a holiday but can't think of anywhere he'd like to go. He asks the disciples for some ideas.
"How about Mars?" asks one.
"No chance!" says God. "I went there about 20,000 years ago and it was dusty and boring!
"Or Pluto then?" asks another.
"Ooh no thanks, I tried there about 12,000 years ago and it was freezing!"
"Well why not give Earth a visit then?" asks a third disciple.
"Forget that!" says God. "I went there 2,000 years ago, got some bird up the duff and they're still harping on about it now!"

When times are tough, share a joke, have a laugh and fight on! Thank you for all that you do for us back home.

Claire Wilson

An Eskimo has broken down so he calls an Eskimo mechanic. The mechanic arrives and takes a quick look under the bonnet.

"Ah, I see," says the mechanic "You've blown a seal."

"No," replies the Eskimo wiping his mouth, "it's just frost!"

For all who serve in the British Army – the best! Stay safe.

Phil Bull

Private X is called in to the platoon sergeant's office, where he is given a brown A4 envelope and an Army-issue fire axe by the sergeant. The private is told to report to CSM HQ Coy, deliver the envelope and axe and await a reply.

Private X marches smartly off and arrives at CSM's office, knocks, enters and stands to attention in front of the desk.

CSM looks up and Private X delivers the envelope, whilst maintaining a proper grip on the fire axe.

CSM opens the envelope and finds a sheet of A4 paper with this written on it . . .

"GIVE ME THE DAY OFF – OR I'LL CHOP YOUR FUCKING BALLS OFF WITH THIS AXE, YOU FAT BASTARD."

The British fighting man – best in the world! Thanks for proving it again and again.

Tim, Ex 2 Para 1982

A woman bursts into her boss's office and demands that he investigate a colleague for sexual harassment.

"OK, calm down and tell me what happened." says her boss.

"James said that my hair smelled nice!" she shrieks.

"Well I don't see what's so wrong with that!" says the now confused boss.

"Sir," replies the woman, now in tears, "James is a midget!"

Dave "Jonno" Johnson, Ex RN

This guy walks into a pub in Norwich and orders a white wine. Everybody sitting around the bar looks up, surprised.
The landlord looks around and says "You're not from round here, are you . . . where you from fella?"
The guy says, "I'm from London."
The landlord asks, "What do you do in London?"
The guy responds, "I'm a taxidermist."
The landlord asks, "A taxidermist . . . now what is a taxidermist?"
The guy says "I mount animals."
The landlord grins and shouts out to the whole pub, "It's OK everyone, he's one of us!"

Keep your chins up! We're all thinking of you here!

Dave Calmont

A flat-chested woman buys a magic mirror and hangs it on her bedroom door. One evening, while getting undressed, she playfully says, "Mirror, mirror on my door, make my tits a forty-four."
Instantly her tits grow to enormous proportions. She runs to tell her husband what has happened.
He immediately rushes to the mirror and drops his trousers. He crosses his fingers and says, "Mirror, mirror on the door, make my penis touch the floor!"
There's a bright flash . . . and his legs fall off.

Utrinque Paratus!

Mark Spring

A young boy goes to the zoo with his father. As they are passing the elephant exhibit, the youngster looks over at the elephant.

After a few seconds he turns to his dad and asks, "Dad, what's that hanging down from the elephant?"

His father replies "That's his trunk, son."

"No, no, dad," says the boy, "at the back."

"Oh, that's his tail." replies his father.

"No, dad," the boy says, "Between his legs."

The father looks over and replies "That's his penis, son."

The young lad thinks about the answer for a minute, and then says to his father, "Last week, mummy told me that was nothing."

"Well son," replies his father, "You have to remember that your mother is a very spoiled woman."

With love, pride and respect. Stay safe.

Jo Clarke

How can you tell if your wife is dead?
The sex is the same but the dishes pile up.

Per Mare, Per Terram.

MJ

A ventriloquist does his usual run of silly blonde jokes when a big blonde woman in the fourth row stands on her chair and says, "Oi! I've heard just about enough of your blonde jokes. What makes you think you can stereotype women that way? What do a person's physical attributes have to do with their worth as a human being? It's guys like you who keep women like me from being respected at work and in my community, of reaching my full potential as a person."

Flustered, the ventriloquist begins to apologize, when the blonde interrupts him: "You stay out of this, I'm talking to that little fucker on your knee!"

Thank you to each and every one of you for your service.

Chris Robinson, married to a blonde for 22 years

Two guys were swapping stories in the park one day and one guy mentioned that during the war he was captured and held for weeks without food.

The other guy asked, "How could you survive without food?"

"It wasn't easy," he said. "But I had a big meal before I was captured and learned to eat my own shit."

"WHAT? That's disgusting!" said the first guy. "I don't believe you!"

Without a second thought, the man reached into his pants, shit into his hand and promptly ate it.

The second guy said, "My God! If you can do that so easily, we can bet big money and make some serious cash!"

"Sounds good to me," said the man "I'm skint."

The next day the guy made a bet with two wealthy men he knew.

"No one can eat their own shit." said one of the wealthy men.

The war veteran did what he did the previous day and shat in his hand. He put it on his lap and looked down ready to dig in, when all of a sudden he was violently sick across the room.

The wealthy gamblers take their winnings and leave, furious that they have had their time wasted but happy with their win.

"We lost it all!" said the veteran's friend. "Why didn't you eat the shit?"

"There was a hair in it!" said the veteran.

I hope your rations are better out there! Stay safe.

Pete Vine

185

A couple were in their bedroom and the girl says to her boyfriend, "I wish I had bigger tits." The boyfriend says, 'Well I recommend you get some toilet tissue and rub it between your tits for two months." "How will that help to make my tits bigger?" asks the girlfriend. "Well, it worked for your ass." says the boyfriend.

Hang in there, guys and gals. Everyone in the UK is VERY proud of you all!

Mick Dewin

An old couple walk into a hospital. The doctor says to the old man, "I'll need a urine sample, a stool sample, and a blood sample." The old man says, "What?" So the doctor explains again. Once again, the old man says, "What?" So the doctor yells it, "I NEED A URINE SAMPLE, A STOOL SAMPLE, AND A BLOOD SAMPLE!" With that the old woman turns to the old man and says, "He needs your pants!"

Peter Sterling, proud to have served!

What's the difference between love, true love and showing off? Spitting, swallowing and gargling.

Thinking of you all. Keep safe.

Kelly Bryant

A guy goes to his eye doctor for an examination. They start talking as the doctor is examining his eyes. In the middle of their conversation, the doctor casually says, "You need to stop masturbating."
The guy replies, "Why doc? Am I going blind?"
The doctor says, "No, but you've been upsetting the other patients in the waiting room."

With thanks and best wishes.

An ex-blanket stacker

How do you make 5 pounds of fat
look good?
Put a nipple on it.

Swift and Bold!

James

A man walks into a watch and clock store, unzips his trousers and slaps his cock on the counter. The woman behind the counter doesn't bat an eyelid.

She looks him straight in the eye and says, "Put that away Sir, this is a clock shop – not a cock shop!"

"Well," replies the man, "Why don't you put two hands and a face on it?"

To all who have served – THANK YOU!

Daniel Stoner

A female reporter was conducting an interview with a farmer about Mad Cow Disease. "Mr. Brown, do you have any idea what might be the cause of the disease?"
"Sure. Do you know the bulls only screw the cows once a year?"
"Umm, sir, that is a new piece of information, but what's the relationship between this and Mad Cow?"
"And did you know we milk the cows twice a day?" the farmer continues.
"Mr. Brown, that's interesting, but what's your point?"
"Lady, the point is this: if I'm playing with your tits twice a day, but only fucking you once a year, wouldn't you go mad, too?"

I cannot find the words to express my pride and gratitude for what you all do for us. Keep safe and come home soon!

Len Carlton

How do you stop a woman sucking your cock?
Marry her!

Mark Timpson

A little girl goes to see Santa Claus at the local shopping centre. When she sits down on Santa's lap Santa asks, "What do you want for Christmas, little girl?"

"I want a Barbie and a GI Joe." says the little girl.

"But Barbie comes with Ken." Santa says.

"No, Barbie only 'cums' with GI Joe!"

For all in the Signals Regt. Keep safe!

Malcolm Holden

A man is lying in bed in the hospital with an oxygen mask over his mouth. A young nurse appears to sponge his hands and feet.

"Nurse," he mumbles from behind the mask, "Are my testicles black?"

Embarrassed, the young nurse replies, "I don't know, I'm only here to wash your hands and feet."

He struggles again to ask, "Nurse, are my testicles black?"

Finally, she pulls back the covers, raises his gown, holds his penis in one hand and his testicles in her other hand and takes a close look, and says "There is nothing wrong with them!"

Finally, the man pulls off his oxygen mask and replies, "That was very nice but, are . . . my . . . test . . . results . . . back?"

Jimbo, Ex RGJ

A little boy and a little girl were playing in the woods.

The little girl asked the boy, "What is a penis?"

The boy replied, "I don't know."

At that time he hears his mum calling him for lunch. He goes home and eats his lunch. Then he sees his dad on the couch. He goes up to his dad and ask him, "What is a penis?" The dad whips his out and says to the boy, "This is a penis, as a matter of fact this is the perfect penis." The boy leaves to go find his friend and brings her to the woods. The girl again asks him what a penis is. He whips out his penis and says to her, "This is a penis, and if it was two inches smaller it would be the perfect penis!"

Proud of all of you and the great job you do in serving our country. Thank you.

Dawn Peacock

What's the difference between a pickpocket and a peeping Tom? A pickpocket snatches watches.

Peter Vine

A woman arrived at a party. While scanning the guests, she spotted an attractive man standing alone.

She approached him, smiled and said, "Hello. My name is Carmen."

"That's a beautiful name," he replied. "Is it a family name?"

"No," she replied, "as a matter of fact I gave it to myself. It represents the things that I enjoy the most – cars and men. Therefore I chose Carmen. What's your name?"

He answered "B. J. Titsengolf."

Enjoy guys. Thanks for keeping us safe.

Darren Fields

A man is sitting in a bar when a beautiful woman walks up and whispers in his ear, "I'll do anything you want for £50."
He puts his drink down and starts going through his pockets. He pulls a load of notes and change and manages to find £50.
He hands the handful of cash to the woman and says, "Here . . . paint my fucking house."

For my son. Proud of you all.

David March

A gynaecologist had a burning desire to change careers and become a mechanic. So she found out from her local tech college what was involved, signed up for evening classes and attended diligently, learning all she could. When time for the practical exam approached, she prepared carefully for weeks, and completed the exam with tremendous skill. When the results came back, she was surprised to find that she had obtained a mark of 150%.

Fearing an error, she called the instructor, saying, "I don't want to appear ungrateful for such an outstanding result, but I wondered if there had been an error which needed adjusting."

The instructor said, "During the exam, you took the engine apart perfectly, which was worth 50% of the total mark. You put the engine back together again perfectly, which is also worth 50% of the mark. I gave you an extra 50% because you did all of it THROUGH the exhaust!"

Thank you so much for all that you do for our safety and those in danger where you are.

Susan Thomas

A general and an admiral were sitting in the barbershop. Following their shaves, the barber reached for some aftershave to slap on their faces.

The admiral shouted, "Hey, don't put that stuff on me! My wife will think I've been in a whorehouse!" The General turned to the barber and said, "Go ahead and put it on. My wife doesn't know what the inside of a whorehouse smells like."

Anon

Perhaps one of the most interesting and colourful words in the English language today is the word "fuck". It is the one magical word that, just by its sound, can describe pain, pleasure, love and hate. In language, "fuck" falls into many grammatical categories.

It can be used as a verb, both transitive (John fucked Mary) and intransitive (Mary was fucked by John). It can be an action verb (John really gives a fuck); a passive verb (Mary really doesn't give a fuck); an adverb (Mary is fucking interested in John); or as a noun (Mary is a terrific fuck). It can also be used as an adjective (Mary is fucking beautiful); or an interjection (Fuck! I'm late for my date with Mary). It can even be used as a conjunction (Mary is easy, fuck she's also stupid).

As you can see, there are very few words with the overall versatility of the word "fuck".

Aside from its sexual connotations, this incredible word can be used to describe many situations:

1. Greetings: "How the fuck are ya?"
2. Fraud: "I got fucked by the car dealer."
3. Resignation: "Oh, fuck it!"
4. Trouble: "I guess I'm fucked now."

5. Aggression: "FUCK YOU!"
6. Disgust: "Fuck me."
7. Confusion: "What the fuck . . . ?"
8. Difficulty: "I don't understand this fucking business!"
9. Despair: "Fucked again . . . "
10. Pleasure: "I fucking couldn't be happier."
11. Displeasure: "What the fuck is going on here?"
12. Lost: "Where the fuck are we."
13. Disbelief: "UNFUCKINGBELIEVABLE!"
14. Retaliation: "Up your fucking ass!"
15. Denial: "I didn't fucking do it."
16. Perplexity: "I know fuck all about it."
17. Apathy: "Who really gives a fuck, anyhow?"
18. Greetings: "How the fuck are ya?"
19. Suspicion: "Who the fuck are you?"
20. Panic: "Let's get the fuck out of here."
21. Directions: "Fuck off."
22. Disbelief: "How the fuck did you do that?"

It has also been used by many notable people throughout history:
"Where did all these fucking Indians come from?"
– General Custer

"Where the fuck is all this water coming from?" – Captain of the Titanic

"That's not a real fucking gun."
– John Lennon

"Who's gonna fucking find out?"
– Richard Nixon

"Any fucking idiot could understand that."
– Albert Einstein

"It does so fucking look like her!"
– Picasso

"How the fuck did you work that out?"
– Pythagoras

"You want what on the fucking ceiling?"
– Michaelangelo

"Fuck a duck."
– Walt Disney

"Why? Because it's fucking there!"
– Edmund Hilary

"I don't suppose it's gonna fucking rain?"
– Joan of Arc

"Scattered fucking showers, my ass."
– Noah

With deepest respect for you all. Hang tough.

An American colleague

Three rottweilers were in the vet's waiting room. One asks the other two why they are there?

The first says, "I was out for a walk when a thug attacked my master, so I ripped the thug's throat out and killed him. They're putting me down today."

The second says, "A burglar broke into the house while my master was out, so I attacked the burglar and bit his arm off. They're putting me down today too."

The third says, "I was patrolling the house one night, and I wandered into the bathroom to find my master's wife naked and bending over the bath, so I jumped up and gave her one from behind!"

The other two look at him and say, "And they're putting you down for that?"

"Oh no," says the third dog, "She's brought me in to have my claws clipped!"

Respect and thanks to you all.

Eric Jones